aspects
of
english

THE RESEARCH PAPER

Robert Hamilton Moore

HOLT, RINEHART AND WINSTON

NEW YORK · TORONTO · LONDON · SYDNEY

THE AUTHOR

Robert Hamilton Moore, Professor of English Composition, The George Washington University, has written a number of well-known college textbooks, including *Effective Writing,* now in its third edition. Dr. Moore is a member of the Executive Committee of the College Conference on Composition and Communication and is past president of the Middle Atlantic College English Association.

89   008   1514131211

Copyright © 1967 by Holt, Rinehart and Winston, Inc.

Another version of this material was published as part
of *Effective Writing,* Third Edition copyright © 1965
by Holt, Rinehart and Winston, Inc.

Printed in the United States of America

ISBN 0-03-064865-3

CONTENTS

THE RESEARCH PAPER

A very important part of your work in English composition is that dealing with the research paper, or the "library paper," or the "source paper," or the "term paper"—all names for the same project.

Until now, you have focused your attention on expressing your own ideas, re-creating your own experience, passing your painfully acquired knowledge on to others who might be saved some of your pain as a result. But the human race has been acquiring knowledge, often at the price of intolerable pain, for many thousands of years. One of the major purposes of the research paper project is to teach you how to get at the experience and knowledge of the men who have gone before you, who have observed and thought and recorded what they have learned just so you could make use of it. The libraries of the world are full of knowledge that you can put to good use if you know how to find it. The research paper project is primarily an introduction to the best ways to find out what the race has already learned.

Another purpose is to give you a chance to learn how to manage really complicated problems of organization and expression in a long paper whose material has come from many sources representing many points of view, about which you have a chance to exercise your own intelligence in weighing, selecting, rejecting, and shaping the material into a final form of your own—perhaps as a new and significant judgment, certainly as a new and original organization, phrasing, and evaluation of what is known about your topic.

Still another purpose is to give you practice in critical reading. You will find printed sources which sound equally authoritative. Yet some will be sadly ignorant, or out of date, or fanatically "riding a thesis" so that any evidence of whatever sort is interpreted with prejudice and warped into position in the imposing edifice the writers have decided in advance to build. Or you will find sources whose authors are honestly and sincerely and intelligently trying to find the truth; yet these authors will disagree violently. It is enlightening and valuable to learn to judge for yourself and to evaluate what you read.

And most practical of all, a final purpose is to teach you what to do if you go on to college and a professor announces that you will be required to write a term paper, which may determine much of your grade in the course.

At this point you may be thinking, "This job will be easy. I've got two or three books at home on the subject that I'll write on, and I remember an article about it in *Life*. I can patch together something over the weekend." Forget it. The details and possible interpretations involved in the search for truth on any subject are too complex for two or three books and any popular magazines to clarify. Writing a research paper is not an exercise in patching together, but in digging.

THE USE OF THE LIBRARY

For thousands of years, the human race has been storing up its collective wisdom in libraries. No two libraries are exactly alike. The region in which a library is located, the interests of its donors or its directors, the accumulated results of losses and acquisitions —all these factors make the collection of any one library different from that of any other. Your library's share of "the best that has been thought and said in the world," however, will give you quite enough raw material for your research paper. It is obvious that you do not have time or energy to read all the books, magazines, newspapers, pamphlets, and manuscripts your library contains in the hope of stumbling on facts or opinions which have a bearing on a particular subject you are interested in; but, fortunately, you do not have to. Even though the collection of each library is unique, the machinery by which you can search that collection for material you can use is standardized. The same research tools and methods can be used in any library in the country. Standard reference books, catalogues, and indexes save you from having to guess where to look for material, or from having to wonder what your library owns and what it lacks.

The Card Catalogue

The card catalogue—rows of filing cabinets filled with three-by-five-inch cards listing every book in the library's collection, usually in three different ways—is an invaluable aid to research. From it can be found what *books* the library contains, alphabetically listed by the author's name, the first important word of the title, and the subjects treated. Whether or not the student has direct access to the book stacks, a knowledge of the card catalogue is essential.

The basic card is the author card, printed by the Library of Congress and distributed to libraries all over the country.

E
175.9
.S34
1934   **Schlesinger, Arthur Meier,** 1888–
New viewpoints in American history, by Arthur Meier
Schlesinger...New York, The Macmillan company, 1934.
x p., 21., 299 p.   20½ cm.
Originally published 1922.
"Bibliographical note" at end of each chapter.
CONTENTS.—The influence of immigration on American history.—
Geographic factors in American development.—Economic influences
in American history.—The decline of aristocracy in America.—Radical-
ism and conservatism in American history.—The role of women in
American history.—The American revolution.—Economic aspects of
the movement for the Constitution.—The significance of Jacksonian
democracy.—The state rights fetish.—The foundations of the modern
era.—The riddle of the parties.
1. U. S.—Hist.—Philosophy. 2. U. S.—Hist. 3. U. S. Pol. govt.
I. Title.
                                                    34–25367
Library of Congress   E175.9.S34   1934
                                                    973.04
                        [3]

The typed number in the upper left-hand corner is the "call number," the number by which the librarian knows where in the stacks of books the particular volume is shelved. It is not important that you understand how the librarian arrives at that number, but it is extremely important that you copy it down exactly and completely as you fill out a "call slip" for a book. If you do not, you will have to go back to the card catalogue and get it.[1]

The first line of the printed card gives you the author's name, surname first, and the dates of his birth and, unless he was living when the card was printed, his death.

Second is the title of the book (with only the first word and proper names capitalized), the author's name as it appears on the title page, the edition (if other than the first), and the facts of publication, that is, the place of publication, the publisher, and the date.

In your final paper you will need that information; consequently you should note carefully everything offered in the first two elements of the catalogue card.

The rest of the information provided by the card does not appear in your final paper. But do not, on that account, ignore it. From the third item you can get an idea of the size of the book— how many pages and how large a volume. You can tell whether or not it contains illustrations, maps, charts, or a bibliography that might be useful to you, and even sometimes how many times it has been reprinted.

Even more important is the fourth item (which, unfortunately, does not often appear), the analysis of the contents. If that analysis is given, it will tell you at once whether or not the book will touch your particular phase of the general subject the book deals with.

Next—and again very important to you—are the subject headings under which the book has been classified. This element of the card will often suggest related subjects that should be consulted and will give you key terms to keep in mind as you consult not only the card catalogue but also the other kinds of indexes to library material.

Finally, there are a series of numerical entries that are useful chiefly to librarians—the Library of Congress call number (which will also be listed in the upper left-hand corner if your library uses the Library of Congress system), the Dewey Decimal classification number (which will be listed as the call number if your library

---

[1] If you wish to know more about the classification systems, study any one of several good handbooks on library practice which your librarian recommends.

follows that system), the Library of Congress card number, the copyright number, and so on.

Most books are listed not only by author but also by title and subject. From whichever angle you approach the card catalogue, you will get clues that will lead you to book sources. You should, however, follow up the other avenues of approach besides the one you first took. Usually, for example, you will begin with subject cards. But you should remember to look also at the author cards of an authority who turns up frequently; there may be other books of his bearing on the subject which the library has neglected to list under that particular subject heading. The subject headings are rather specific—history, for example, touches and overlaps many other concepts. They must be used intelligently and imaginatively, because your material may be scattered widely. Check related subject headings; they may lead you to useful sources. And use the cross-reference cards suggesting other ways of cataloguing related material, or use the *Library of Congress Subject Headings*, a ready-made cross-reference volume. A "see" card or a "see also" card should never be ignored. The first indicates that you are consulting the catalogue through a key term the library does not use and tells you what term to look for; the second suggests a closely related subject heading that may provide important additional material.

One source of material is often overlooked—biography. It may not be filed under any other subject matter heading, so that such a major source, say, as Freeman's four-volume *R. E. Lee* may not appear at all under U.S.—History—Civil War. Yet Volumes II and III are at least as important as Freeman's *Lee's Lieutenants*. Be sure to check biographical material for people who are importantly involved with your topic.

A few remarks might be made about the ways in which librarians file the catalogue cards. A little browsing in the catalogue will do more to teach you than any amount of direct advice, but some helpful hints may be offered.

Books *by* a writer are filed before books *about* him.

Abbreviations are filed as if they were written out in full— *U.S.* comes where *United States* would come. *Mac, Mc,* and *M'* are all filed as if they were *Mac.* Numerals are filed as if they were spelled out. *Von* and *de* are ignored, and the last name is used instead, as in *Rochambeau, Comte de,* or *Steuben, Baron Friedrich Wilhelm von.*

Single key words in phrases come before compounds, or, as the librarian phrases it, "short comes before long."

Slave labor	Slavery
Slave songs	Slavery and abolition
Slave-trade	Slavery and the church

Historical subdivisions are arranged chronologically; otherwise subdivisions of a topic are arranged alphabetically.

U.S.—History—Colonial Period
U.S.—History—King William's War, 1689–1697
U.S.—History—King George's War, 1744–1748
U.S.—History—French and Indian War, 1755–1763
U.S.—History—Revolution

But

Slave-trade
Slave-trade, Africa, West
Slave-trade, Brazil
Slave-trade, History
Slave-trade, U.S.
Slave-trade, West Indies

Follow through the listings under all possible subject headings before you decide the library contains no books dealing with your topic (including general books overlapping the topic).

Periodical Indexes

Magazine articles provide much of our current reading, but magazine articles are not listed in the card catalogues, though the magazines themselves will be. To find articles which have appeared in magazines or in other publications issued periodically, you can use the many periodical indexes. Every student should be aware of the major indexes: *Poole's Index to Periodical Literature* (indexing many periodicals published during the nineteenth century), the *Readers' Guide to Periodical Literature* (a more useful index covering popular magazines of the period from 1900 to the present), the *Social Science & Humanities Index* (formerly the *International Index,* on scholarly articles in the humanities and the social sciences), the *Industrial Arts Index* (engineering and business), and the many specialized indexes covering the student's particular interest. The last two, and the specialized indexes which can include more periodicals since they try to cover less ground, are especially important. *Never* stop with the *Readers' Guide.* It indexes the popular magazines on the newsstands, and the authors of the feature articles listed in it are very likely to have acquired what they know by the same process of library research that you are learning. They are professional writers, but amateurs in the subject matter. Like them, you need to consult the experts, whose contributions are in the professional journals and the scholarly books.

As you use any of the periodical indexes, be sure that you understand the system they follow. Consult the explanatory material at the front of the volumes for full discussion of their abbreviations, the order of details, and so on. You will later see that you need to record all bibliographical material according to a specialized system conventionally followed in research papers. Before you can translate an index entry into the system you must use, you must understand both systems thoroughly.

Newspaper and Pamphlet Indexes

Most newspapers are not indexed, but since most papers print the same news on the same day, two particular newspaper indexes can be used to locate news stories in nearly any paper. One is *The New York Times Index,* and the other is *The* (London) *Times Index.*

Pamphlets are less completely indexed, but two indexes are very useful, as far as they go. The *Vertical File Service Catalog* indexes much pamphlet material and should be consulted. The *Document Catalogue* and the subsequent *Monthly Catalogue* list many government publications.

Specialized Indexes

There are many specialized indexes of various kinds and of varying value; among them are the following:

>   *Agricultural Index*
>   *Art Index*
>   *Book Review Digest*
>   *Chemical Abstracts*

> *Dramatic Index*
> *Education Index*
> *Engineering Index*
> *Index to Legal Periodicals*
> *Index Medicus*
> *Modern Humanities Research Association Bibliographies*
> *Psychological Abstracts*
> *Public Affairs Information Service*

Make use of any specialized indexes available; you can locate them by consulting Winchell, *Guide to Reference Books,* Robert W. Murphy, *How and Where to Look It Up,* the *Bibliographic Index,* or—after you have really looked for yourself—the librarians.

Reference Books

Reference books, like the telephone directory, are designed to be consulted for specific and classified information about limited subjects. The periodical indexes we have just been considering are reference books, and there are many others, some of which, like the general dictionaries, are already familiar to you. Among the most important are the encyclopedias, the dictionaries, the biographical dictionaries, the yearbooks, and the atlases.

GENERAL ENCYCLOPEDIAS: General encyclopedias attempt to present objective and authoritative articles on as many topics of general interest as possible. Because they differ, of necessity, one from another and edition from edition, it is well to consult several rather than only one. Among the best edited and most dependable are the following:

> *Encyclopedia Americana* and its annual supplement *The Americana Annual*
> *Encyclopaedia Britannica* and its annual supplement *The Britannica Book of the Year*
> *Collier's Encyclopedia* (This is designed primarily for high school use and will often provide a good introductory article from which you can—and should—go on to the adult encyclopedias listed above.)

It is usually best to use the latest available editions, which will present the results of the most recent scholarship. Only if you wish to know what was thought about a given topic at an earlier period (or if your topic has been dropped from late editions) should you consult an edition other than the most recent one.

DICTIONARIES: In addition to the standard unabridged dictionaries,

> *The New Century Dictionary of the English Language*
> *Funk & Wagnall's New Standard Dictionary of the English Language*
> *Webster's Third New International Dictionary of the English Language,*

every student should be aware of two or three comprehensive historical dictionaries.

> *Dictionary of American English on Historical Principles*
> Mitford M. Mathews, *Dictionary of Americanisms*
> *Oxford English Dictionary on Historical Principles* (also called the *New English Dictionary* or the *Murray Dictionary)*

These multivolumed dictionaries are invaluable in tracing the development and change of meanings and in determining what a word may have meant to an author writing in an earlier time—the Anglican *Book of Common Prayer,* for example, in praying, "Prevent us, O Lord, in all our doings," is confusing until you understand the sixteenth-century use of *prevent.*

BIOGRAPHICAL DICTIONARIES: At least four biographical dictionaries should be familiar to every student, and there are many others in specialized fields.

> *Dictionary of American Biography,* and supplement
> *Dictionary of National Biography* (British), and supplements
> *Who's Who in America*
> *Who's Who* (British)

The first two are concerned with prominent persons no longer living, the second two with prominent living persons.

YEARBOOKS: Yearbooks contain valuable factual information about events of each year. There are many, but among the most important are the following:

The Americana Annual
The Britannica Book of the Year
American Year Book
Facts on File
New International Year Book
World Almanac and Book of Facts

ATLASES: The three best-known atlases are the following:

Encyclopaedia Britannica World Atlas
Columbia Lippincott Gazetteer of the World
Rand McNally Commercial Atlas and Marketing Guide

Early in your work on the research paper you should familiarize yourself with the very important general reference works that have been listed. In addition, you should examine carefully the specialized periodical indexes, biographical dictionaries, technical dictionaries, and encyclopedias offering information about your special field of study. Consult Winchell, *Guide to Reference Books* or some similar guide (there are many), browse through the library reference room, and consult the reference librarian. Remember that she should not be expected to do your work for you, but part of her job is to know the best reference sources for specialized investigations. Make use of her expert knowledge.

E X E R C I S E S

A. What would be the best source to consult if you wished to find the following information?
   1. A list of the principal books by Sir Winston Churchill.
   2. The tonnage of steel produced last year in the United States.
   3. The career of Francis Scott Key.
   4. A sketch of the early history of Jamaica.
   5. The approximate date at which *prevent* appeared in print with its modern meaning.

6. The philosophical publications of Herbert Spencer, who lived in England from 1820 to 1903.
7. The location and height of Mount Everest.
8. Articles in historical periodicals, between 1950 and 1960, on King Richard III of England.
9. Newspaper accounts of the death of Ernest Hemingway in 1961.
10. Specialized encyclopedias in religion and ethics.

(If you go to the library to look up the information, handle the reference books carefully. When many students look up the same items, books wear out rapidly.)

B. Prepare and submit to your teacher a list of the specialized encyclopedias, specialized periodical indexes, and specialized biographical dictionaries necessary to anyone doing research in the field in which you expect to write your paper.

C. After careful examination of the books, write out and submit to your teacher a brief statement of the content and scope of the following: *Oxford English Dictionary, Cambridge History of English Literature,* Bartlett's *Familiar Quotations, Book Review Digest, Webster's Biographical Dictionary,* Winchell, *Guide to Reference Books.*

D. Consult your library's card catalogue to discover how many books your library contains from which you could secure detailed information about Lady Jane Grey. Include in your list biographies, specialized histories of the period, and the pertinent volumes of general histories. Follow up all "see" and "see also" cross-references.

RESEARCH PAPER PROCEDURE

Selecting a Subject

When your teacher announces that the time has come to begin the research paper project, you need first to find an answer to the question of what to write about.

If you are given a choice—and many teachers, for a number of good reasons, prefer to assign topics—you should select a topic you are interested in. For one thing, you will find the task more pleasant if you are interested in the topic from the first. Almost any subject will become interesting as you learn more and more about it, but initial interest will help carry you through the chores of preparing the preliminary bibliography and doing the preliminary reading. You might select a topic you already know a little about, or you might take this opportunity to investigate a subject you have always wanted to study but never have had time for.

First, of course, your subject should be one which cannot be settled from a single source. The process of making steel in a Bessemer converter is not a research topic. All explanations will be essentially the same. Choose a topic than can teach you what the library project is designed to teach.

Second, your topic, obviously, should not be too big. An assignment to write a two- to five-thousand-word paper may be appalling at the outset, but you will soon find, as you begin to learn more and more about the topic, that a surprisingly little bit goes a long way. In order to give yourself a chance to develop your subject as fully as your new knowledge will allow, you must limit, subdivide, pare, and prune your subject until you have a chance to learn it thoroughly and really say something useful about it. Stone Age man? Too big, too vague, and too widespread. Aurignacian man in France? Better, but still too big. The religious beliefs of Aurignacian man? Still too big, by the time the ramifications are covered. The cave paintings? Possible, but it would slip over into the religious beliefs and get out of hand. The cave paintings of Lascaux? That might be about right. If it proved to be still too big, the paper could be restricted still further—to the discovery, say, or to the precautions taken to preserve the paintings from tourists and fresh air. One good way to find a limited topic is to notice points which a general article on the subject treats with only incidental comment. An article on the Tower of London, for example, touching on many events in its nine hundred years of history, mentions "the notorious theft of the English crown by Thomas Blood." The Tower of London is too big a topic, but many subtopics that catch your interest will turn up even in a brief account. Your final choice will depend partly on the material you find available in your library. But remember to select a topic small enough to be suitable for working on. As you do early reading, focus on smaller and smaller aspects of your general subject until you settle on a topic you can handle in the time and space at your disposal.

Also, for various reasons, the topic you decide to investigate should not be too new, or too technical, or too regional, or too controversial. Let us consider each of these limitations in turn.

Your topic should not be too new. A major purpose of the project is to teach you to use the facilities of the library, and libraries are chiefly collections of books and magazines. Your subject, then, must be old enough to have had time to get into book and magazine form. The exciting news story on the front page of today's newspaper would make a poor subject; the sources would be largely newspaper stories and columnists' speculations. Not only would it be hard to locate pertinent material, but many libraries are reluctant to have too many people handle their flimsy newspaper files until they have been microfilmed, and you would be limited then to a very few papers. Again, too new a subject would be one, of whatever age, that has not been studied by experts in primary research. (Primary sources are letters, deeds, wills, bills of lading, and so on and so on.) It is not always chronological age that counts here. Douglas Southall Freeman, for example, found as he began to work on his biography of Washington that nobody ever had bothered to study plantation life along the Potomac in the days of Washington's youth. He had to begin with the primary sources before he could write a chapter on the world Washington grew up in. Only by searching the card catalogue and the various indexes can you tell whether a given subject is too new in this sense. And finally, a subject which for one reason or another is being kept secret would be "too new" for your purposes. New processes, commercial secrets, new weapons, new policies—none of them would be open to you. Select a topic old enough to have been treated fully in books and articles.

For quite different reasons, your topic should not be too technical. A report on a technical subject for a nontechnical audience is hard to write, but that is no real objection; the practice would be good for you, and as *The New York Times* or *Time* or many other exemplars demonstrate, success is perfectly possible. But if the subject is too technical for you to understand yourself, the problem becomes important. Medical subjects, for example, are often discussed only in the professional medical journals and only in medical jargon. Unless you already know the terminology doctors use in talking to each other, you may be wholly unable to make sense of your sources, and you have too little time to preface your research with a course in medical terminology. The material is there, but as far as you are concerned, it might as well not be there at all. The same difficulty arises with a topic on which much of the material is in a foreign language you cannot read.

A regional subject might be excellent if you are yourself in the right region. A history of Jefferson County, Kentucky, for example, might be written in Louisville. But it might be very difficult to find much material if the same topic were tried in Kansas, in a library which might have almost no material at all on Jefferson County, Kentucky. Library collections, remember, differ greatly. Check the card catalogue and the periodical indexes before rejecting a regional topic, but do not be surprised if you discover that little material is available. It would be better to choose another topic than to go to the expense in money and time to arrange for interlibrary loans or to travel to the distant libraries where your material is stored. The research scholar often must do that, but you can learn library research and term-paper methods just as well with a topic that can be handled right at home.

Finally, the subject should not be too controversial. Avoid topics on which you yourself have violent prejudices. You need to learn to get rid of such prejudices, or at least to base them on valid evidence and clear thought; but the library research paper is perhaps not the best place in which to do that. Again, be sure the topic is one in which truth, or a high degree of probability, can be found. Do not, for example, set out to discover by means of library research which of the two and seventy jarring sects represent true Christianity, nor, for that matter, which philosophical definition of Truth itself is the true one.

Your teacher may suggest further limitations. Here we need to consider only one more: To get the greatest good from the assignment, it is well to select a subject which will allow you to produce a *judgment* rather than a mere *report*. A judgment is a paper in which you can reach conclusions of your own after thoughtfully evaluating all the evidence. One of the fascinating problems of American history, for example, concerns the final career of Aaron Burr, who had been Thomas Jefferson's Vice-President and, but for Alexander Hamilton, would probably have been President in Jefferson's stead. What was his scheme to detach the Lower Mississippi country from the United States? He was acquitted in his trial for treason. From the evidence, available then or since uncovered, should he have been acquitted? Did he himself really know what he intended to do? What is the evidence and how do you think it should be interpreted? Such a subject gives you a chance not only to write a good paper, but even to write a brilliant one.

A report, on the other hand, is well worth doing, but it can never be brilliant. It deals with a purely factual topic and consists of a clear presentation of all the facts, offering no opinion because facts do not admit opinion; they are either true or false. A report could be written, for example, on Aaron Burr's conspiracy, indicating merely what occurred, who was involved, and how the trial went; but the topic almost demands an evaluation of the evidence and an attempt to explain Burr's actions. If you agree that the second would be a more valuable paper, you will see why your teacher may well feel that a judgment is superior to a report.

In summary, ask yourself, first, what subjects you are most interested in and would most like to study. Limit your choice to a topic small enough to handle. Avoid the too new, the too technical, the too regional, the too controversial. And if you wish to show what you really can do, and if you wish, incidentally, to learn as much from the assignment as possible, select a topic which will allow you to form your own opinions of the meaning of your material.

Once your topic has been selected, you are ready to go to the library.

EXERCISE

Submit to your teacher for his comments a list of six carefully restricted topics on which you would like to do research. Explain briefly why you are interested in each topic and why you believe it would be a good subject for a research paper.

Preparing a Preliminary Bibliography

The next job is to find out what material on your subject is available in your library. For that task, you need to make up a preliminary bibliography, listing, in a form that will later be very convenient, the books and the articles which from their titles look promising.

The tools for this, of course, are the card catalogue, the general and specialized periodical indexes, and any specialized bibliographies you may be able to find. But before you begin to record authors and titles, go to the reference room and read a good encyclopedia article on your subject. One of the well-edited, up-to-date general encyclopedias will be best for most topics, such as the latest edition of the *Britannica* or of the *Americana.* Or if the topic is highly specialized, a more limited encyclopedia may be better, such as the *Encyclopedia of Religion and Ethics* or the *Encyclopedia of the Social Sciences.* There are two good reasons for going first to the encyclopedia: You will get from it an authoritative and objective introduction to the subject, and can from the beginning work with some knowledge of what is important and what is generally known about it; secondly, the encyclopedia will probably give you, at the end of the article, a selected bibliography of the most important sources, and will consequently tell you from the first what books and articles you cannot afford to miss, however much you may be able to add to them. Record all such bibliographical information from the encyclopedia before you turn to the card catalogue and the periodical indexes.

Then comb the card catalogue, following up all cross-references to related subjects. Begin with the subject cards, where all the *books* on your topic should be recorded. Do not forget to note especially books which contain bibliographies and books which are themselves special bibliographies on the subject, all of which will be listed by subject cards. Do not overlook general books on topics which include your subject. If your topic, for example, is the attempt to place Lady Jane Grey on the English throne instead of Mary Tudor, you may find only one or two books on that topic by itself. (Even the Library of Congress lists only thirty-nine.) But the history of England would have been quite different if the plot had succeeded; any general history of England will at least mention it. More limited histories of the Tudor era will give it in more detail. Studies of Mary Tudor or of the Tudor monarchy or of the powerful Dudley family of Northumberland will all provide material. Use the card catalogue intelligently.

Do the same thing with the periodical indexes, both the general indexes, like the *Readers' Guide,* and the specialized indexes, which alone will lead you to the very important detailed articles written by scholars or other experts on your topic. Suppose, for example, you are interested in a literary problem, say the disputed authorship of *Piers Plowman.* There are literally scores of professional publications devoted to literary scholarship, none of which are indexed in the *Readers' Guide* because the *Readers' Guide* is concerned only with magazines aimed at the general reader, and the general reader is not very much interested in the esoteric controversies of literary scholarship. If you wish to find out what scholars think of *Piers Plowman,* you must turn to the *International Index to Periodicals* or the *Modern Humanities Research Association Bibliographies,* which do index professional journals in the humanities. Similarly, a student interested in a medical subject must examine the *Index Medicus,* a chemist must comb *Chemical Abstracts,* and so on. Do not report to your teacher that there is no material available (and do not be satisfied yourself with your preliminary bibliography) until you can honestly say that you have examined all pertinent volumes of the specialized indexes, in addition to the general indexes and the card catalogue. The specialized articles listed may be too technical for you, but at least look at them to make sure.

You should also use, of course, any other bibliographical aids you can find. Be alert to pick up hints from the footnotes of the books and articles you work with. Follow up a reference in the text to any authority who is unfamiliar to you. Check the bibliographies. You are trying to discover what has been written about your topic; be sure nothing important gets by you. You may well find, when you look at a newly discovered book or article, that it is not very useful after all, but you can never know its value until you do look at it.

BIBLIOGRAPHY CARDS: As you find each new possible source, make a careful record of it on a three-by-five-inch card, using a separate card for each item that looks promising. Then you can add to your alphabetical list of sources or withdraw items from it without any of the confusion that would result from trying to keep a helter-skelter list in a notebook.

The purpose of the preliminary bibliography is to give you a convenient list of the sources that might be helpful. After your paper is finished, you will be expected to append a final bibliography which will give your readers a list of the sources you have actually used. It will save time and trouble and will help prevent mistakes if you take down the items for your preliminary bibliography in the form and with the detail you will ultimately need. Your teacher, indeed, will probably examine your bibliography cards to be sure you understand the method, so that care from the beginning not only will save you trouble with the paper itself, but may even save your having to do much of the work over again to satisfy some of the course requirements.

The form of the bibliographical entry differs slightly for each type of source—for books, encyclopedia articles, magazine articles, pamphlets, and unpublished manuscripts, like theses.

But for all types of sources, three bits of information are expected: *author, title, facts of publication.* (The facts of publication are also called the "imprint.") As we shall see, the three-by-five-inch bibliography card recording each source may and often should contain additional information, but those three items are standard. For each source, *take these three items down in full* when you first come across the source and save yourself possible trouble later. And take them down in the recommended form, avoiding abbreviations or other shortcuts.[2]

BOOKS: *Author:* Last name first, to facilitate alphabetizing. If two or three authors are listed on the title page (not the cover or the spine), the book will be alphabetized in your bibliography under the surname of the first author listed. That author's name is given surname first. The names of the other authors, however, are recorded in normal order.

If more than three authors are given on the title page, the first alone is used, and the rest are indicated by *et al.,* meaning "and others."

If the work of many authors has been collected in one volume, as in an anthology, the book is listed under the name of the editor, with his function indicated by the abbreviation *ed.*

An edition of a classic work, or a translation of a foreign work, is listed under the name of the author (unless that name has become almost part of the identifying title, as in Homer's *Iliad*), and the name of the editor or translator follows, identified as *ed.,* or *trans.*

If no author is listed, the book should be listed alphabetically by title. Disregard initial *A* or *The.*

Title: The title of the book, as it appears on the title page, is entered on the second line of the card. If the title is extremely long, it may be shortened, but be sure to include all significant, identifying terms.

[2] The bibliographical forms discussed and illustrated are those of the revised *Style Sheet* of the Modern Language Association with one major modification, the inclusion of the publisher, borrowed from Kate L. Turabian, *A Manual for Writers of Term Papers, Theses, and Dissertations* (Chicago: University of Chicago Press, 1955).

The titles of complete works, like books, are put in italic type by the printer; in longhand or in typing, they are underlined.

Facts of publication: For books, the standard entries are place of publication, publisher, and date. (The date may be given on the title page, or as a copyright date on the back of the title page, or merely as a date appended to a preface or introduction. Use the title page date if one is given.)

All three of the standard entries need to be entered in your bibliography so that a reader who wishes to follow up your references may easily find the same edition (with the same pagination, misprints, revisions, and other details) that you used.

If for any reason one of the three entries cannot be found, indicate that fact by the abbreviations *n.p.* (no place given), *n. pub.* (no publisher), or *n.d.* (no date).

The normal bibliography card for a book by one author looks like this:

> Yarwood, Doreen
>
> The Architecture of England
>
> London: B. J. Batsford, 1963

Examples of the various complexities you are likely to run across follow *in the form the entries should take in your final bibliography.* (On the preliminary cards, author, title, and facts of publication should each be listed on a separate line, as in the sample card above.)

One author:

Yarwood, Doreen. The Architecture of England. London: B. T. Batsford, 1963.

A second work by the same author:

_____. English Costume. London: B. T. Batsford, 1953.
> [The use of a long dash instead of repeating the author's name emphasizes the repetition. In this book the title page uses the abbreviation Co. You may either follow the title page usage, or put all entries in one consistent form, or omit the word altogether.]

Two authors:

Batho, Edith, and Bonamy Dobrée. The Victorians and After. New York: Robert M. McBride Company, 1938.

More than three authors:

Dock, Lavinia, et al. History of American Nursing. New York: The Macmillan Company, 1922.
> [Omitted: Sara Elizabeth Pickett, Clara D. Noyes, Fannie F. Clement, Elizabeth G. Fox, Anna R. van Meter.]

A collection of the work of many authors:

Kreymbourg, Alfred, ed. An Anthology and a History of American Poetry, 2 vols. New York: Tudor Publishing Co., 1930.

An edition other than the first:

Nedham, Carter. Individuality and Conformity, 2nd ed. New York: Arkwrite Company, 1966.

An edition of a classic:

Carlyle, Thomas. Sartor Resartus, ed. by Charles Frederick Harrold. New York: The Odyssey Press, 1937.

A translation of a foreign work:

Zweig, Stefan. Mary Queen of Scotland and the Isles, trans. by Eden and Cedar Paul. New York: The Viking Press, 1935.

Lang, Andrew, Walter Leaf, and Ernest Myers,
    trans. The Iliad of Homer. New York: The
    Modern Library, n.d.
    [The author's name has become so merged with the
    title that the translators are more important in identi-
    fying the edition used.]

A book of more than one volume:

Trevelyan, G. M. History of England, 3 vols.
    Garden City, N.Y.: Doubleday & Company, 1953.

One volume of a set of volumes:

Trevelyan, G. M. History of England, Vol. I.
    Garden City, N.Y.: Doubleday & Company, 1953.

A book in a series:

Faulkner, Harold Underwood. American Political and
    Social History, 4th ed. Crofts American
    History Series, Dixon Ryan Fox, general ed.
    New York: F. S. Crofts & Co., 1946.
    [Notice that this entry also identifies a late edition and
    an editor distinct from the author.]

A book with a "corporate author":

Workers of the Writers' Program of the Work
    Projects Administration. Washington, D.C.:
    A Guide to the Nation's Capital, revised ed.
    American Guide Series. New York: Hastings
    House, 1942.

REFERENCE BOOKS: The following form is suitable for articles
from many kinds of reference books, like the Dictionary of National Biography, as well as from the general encyclopedias.
    Author: As with book entries, put the last name first on the
first line of the bibliography card.
    Many, though not all, encyclopedia articles are signed by the
authors' initials at the end of the article. The authors' full names
are listed at the front or back of the volume, or sometimes of the
first or last volume of a set. If you are certain that the article is not
signed, the first entry on your card cannot be an author entry and
is a title entry instead. But find the author if possible.

Title: The title of the *article,* not of the encyclopedia, is the title of your source. Titles of works which appear as parts of larger wholes, as one article is part of the larger encyclopedia, are put in quotation marks.

Facts of publication: The facts your reader needs before he can understand where your article appeared are the title of the encyclopedia (underlined), the date or edition of the encyclopedia (normally the most recent, unless an earlier edition is somehow superior), the volume number, and the inclusive pages of the article in that volume.

The normal bibliography card for an encyclopedia article looks like this:

> Fraser, Alexander Campbell, and
> Richard Ithamar Aaron
>
> "John Locke"
> Encyclopaedia Britannica (1964),
> XIV, 273-274

The entry would appear in the final bibliography as

Fraser, Alexander Campbell, and Richard Ithamar
Aaron. "John Locke," Encyclopaedia Britannica
(1964), XIV, 273-274.
> [An alternative form, equally acceptable, would enter the date, volume, and pages as: (1964), 14:273-274. Whichever form you adopt, use it consistently.]

MAGAZINE ARTICLES: *Author:* Put the last name first, if the article is signed. If the article is anonymous, alphabetize it under the first key word of the title.

Title: The title of the article is enclosed in quotation marks.

Facts of publication: List the underlined title of the magazine (in full, not abbreviated as it is to save space in the periodical indexes), the volume, the date, and the pages. Two forms are common, as with encyclopedia entries. Whichever form you use, be consistent throughout your bibliography.

If, in addition to numerals representing volume and pages, you need to use numerals representing series, numbers, or sections, identify the numerals by the abbreviations *ser., no., sec., vol.* (or *vols.*), and *p.* (or *pp.*).

The entry would appear in the final bibliography as

```
Viertel, John. "Generative Grammars," College
    Composition and Communication, XV (May,
    1964), 65-81.
        [Or: 15:65-81 (May, 1964).]
```

Many magazine articles, as well as chapters or excerpts from books, are reprinted in anthologies or in casebooks for composition courses. When such reprints are used in research papers, the author and title are, of course, those of the original article or excerpt. If the original facts of publication are indicated, they should also be given in the bibliography. In addition, however, full credit must be given to the immediate source. The result is in effect a double entry.

The normal bibliography card for a magazine article looks like this:

Viertel, John
"Generative Grammars"
College Composition and
        Communication
XV (May, 1964), 65-81.

An excerpt in an anthology:

Becker, Carl L. "The Ideal Democracy," from
Modern Democracy. New Haven, Conn.: Yale
University Press, 1941. Reprinted in Kenneth
L. Knickerbocker, ed. Ideas for Writing, 3rd
ed. New York: Holt, Rinehart and Winston,
Inc., 1962, pp. 318-332.

An article in a casebook:

Reed, Glenn A. "Another Turn on James's The Turn
of the Screw," American Literature,
20:413-423 (January, 1949). Reprinted in
Gerald Willen, ed. A Casebook on Henry
James's "The Turn of the Screw." New York:
T. Y. Crowell Company, 1960, pp. 189-199.

GOVERNMENT PUBLICATIONS: *Author:* Often, no author is
named in government, industrial, and similar publications. If the
author is named, of course his name should be entered, but if the
work is anonymous and the government agency or the corporation
assumes responsibility for it, enter the name of the agency or
corporation as a "corporate author." Use the smallest division of
government that will be recognizable to your reader; the author
card in the card catalogue may or may not help you reach your
decision. Arrange the name to alphabetize the work under the
key term; that is, use Agriculture, United States Department of,
rather than United States Department of Agriculture.

Title: As the title of a complete work, underline it.

Facts of publication: This is often the hardest part of the entry
to determine. Remember that the purpose of the entry is to enable
a reader to secure a copy of the work, and to provide whatever information will be most useful to him. For example, most
federal government publications are printed by the Government
Printing Office, and publications designed for general distribution
are usually available through a branch of the same agency. For
such publications, the Government Printing Office should be
listed as publisher. But if the work is for use within a government
agency, the agency using it should be listed as publisher. If the
publication is one of a series, the titles and numbers of the series
should be given if they will be useful. Dates, when available,
should always be given.

The following examples illustrate a few typical entries:

Commerce, United States Department of. Employee
     Handbook. Washington, D.C.: United States
     Department of Commerce, 1949.

> [No author listed; designed for use in the department.]

Goheen, Howard W., and Samuel Kavruck. Selected
     References on Test Construction, Mental Test
     Theory, and Statistics, 1929-1949.
     Washington, D.C.: United States Government
     Printing Office, 1950.

> [The work is designed for general circulation and may
> be obtained through the Government Printing Office.]

Hall, Milton. Getting Your Ideas Across through
     Writing. Training Manual No. 7. Washington,
     D.C.: Federal Security Agency, 1950.

NEWSPAPER ARTICLES OR NEWS STORIES: *Author:* If the article or news story is signed, the author's name should of course
be recorded. Usually, however, no author is identified, and the
title of the article or story must serve as the first entry.

Title: The title (often no more than a headline or a single topic,
like a name heading an obituary) should be enclosed in quotation
marks, as part of a larger whole.

Facts of publication: The underlined title of the newspaper
(the name of the city is underlined only if it is part of the title of
the paper), the date, the page and section number if the paper has
section numbers, and sometimes the column—all these help the
reader find the articles you are citing. It is often difficult to determine which of several editions is involved. That information
would be useful, because the makeup of newspapers changes
from hour to hour; but the clues to the edition are usually hidden,
and in general the same edition will be distributed to libraries
beyond the immediate place of publication. As a result, editions
are rarely identified in bibliographical citations.

A typical signed newspaper entry would appear like this:

Raskin, A. H. "Steel Talks Wait as Owners Want
     Light on Prices," New York Times, April 1,
     1952, sec. 1, p. 1.

UNPUBLISHED MANUSCRIPTS: University students often have access to specialized treatments of their topics in the form of typed and bound manuscripts prepared as theses for the master's or doctor's degree. These should be consulted if they are available, and of course should be included in the bibliography if they prove useful.

Author and title are always given and should be listed. The title, somewhat oddly, is enclosed in quotation marks even though the work is complete in itself. Since the work is unpublished, there are no "facts of publication," but to let the reader know where the source may be found, it is identified as an unpublished thesis (or dissertation), and the university and the dates are indicated.

A typical thesis entry would appear in the final bibliography like this:

```
Rorabacher, Louise E. "Victorian Women in Life
     and in Fiction." Unpublished thesis, Ph.D.
     (University of Illinois, 1942).
```

Make out a bibliography card for each promising source as you come across it. Take down all the information you will later need in the form you will later need to use. Keep your cards in alphabetical order as you go. The method may seem like a good deal of extra trouble at first, but in the long run it will save time and effort.

ANNOTATING YOUR BIBLIOGRAPHY: At least two additional entries should be made on each card, not for the final bibliography, but for your own working convenience. The first is the library call number by which you may get the book or bound volume of the periodical from the library stacks. When you first locate the item in the card catalogue, enter the call number in a corner of your bibliography card; thus you will save later unnecessary trips back to the card catalogue when you want to withdraw the volume. The second additional entry on the bibliography card is a brief note indicating the value of the source to your paper. When you examine a book or article, make a note of its value on the bibliography card. If you discover, for example, that a source with a promising title is really of no use to you, a note to that effect will save your having to look at it again after you have forgotten what you thought of it. Similarly, a source may give you valuable information without actually providing a single specific detail for your paper; yet a reader following up the subject should know about it. A note on the bibliography card will remind you to include that item in your final bibliography even though you make no direct reference to it in your paper.

The preliminary bibliography, carefully kept, is an invaluable tool. Use it in any way that you can.

EXERCISE

Submit to your teacher the cards on which you have listed your preliminary bibliography. Be sure that you have consulted both general and specialized periodical indexes as well as the card catalogue. Do not overlook pertinent chapters or sections in books covering wider topics.

Making a Tentative Outline

As soon as the preliminary bibliography is well under way—as soon, that is, as you have reaped the ready harvest from the card catalogue and the periodical indexes—it is time to map out the general lines you think the investigation may follow. So far, of course, you know very little about your subject, but you have already read a general encyclopedia article, and as a result you do know something of the main topics your intensive reading will cover; you may even already have glimpsed some of the gaps in your knowledge that you hope to fill.

Before you go any farther, make out a list of the questions you hope finally to be able to answer. They will still be fairly general, but be as specific in phrasing them as you can. Those questions will sketch for you the sections into which your paper will probably fall, and they will help you recognize important items as you read. Suppose, for example, you want to write a paper on Edgar Allan Poe as a literary critic. What questions will your paper eventually have to answer?

1. How much criticism did he write?
2. When?
3. Where did it appear?
4. What critical principles did he follow?

5. How influential was his criticism, that is, what did his contemporaries think of it?
6. What do modern scholars and critics think of his critical work?

There may well be other questions that will occur to you as you work on the problem, or you may find that you have included questions that later prove to be unimportant. But at least you have from the very beginning some sort of framework to build on, and you can always add or subtract questions and expand or contract the questions already asked as your reading goes on.

The next step is an easy one. The questions should be translated into topics which will make up a tentative outline of what you hope to learn as you work. There should also be a clearly phrased statement of what you intend to do, as specifically limited as possible. (Later, a thesis may occur to you, but it cannot be phrased until you have done much of the reading and know where your paper is going.) Just now a clear statement of purpose is enough.

PURPOSE: To find out what critical writing Poe did, and how good it was in the opinion of his contemporaries and of modern scholars.

1. What he wrote
2. When
3. Where
4. His critical principles
5. Contemporary opinion (or influence)
6. Modern opinion

Be prepared at any time to reconsider your tentative outline as your knowledge grows. Here, for example, the first three topics are obviously related, and the three together are less important than any one of the other three. Perhaps the first three topics can be covered in the final paper in a single section—or perhaps other similar items will need to be added. The fourth point in the tentative outline will obviously need to be expanded as you learn more about Poe the critic. You might guess to begin with that he would be highly personal in his criticism, that he would favor romantic writers, and that he would stress esthetics. But that expansion can come as you begin to see what lines he actually followed. Point 5 might grow in the direction of his influence on other writers or in the direction of his contemporary reputation among laymen; it might even prove to be two points before the work is done. The final point may prove less important than you expect.

But with the tentative outline as a guide, you can direct your reading from the first. As a book or article on Poe touches Poe the critic, you will not only know that here is something you need to make notes on, but even know what use you may be able to make of the information. Your note-taking, in other words, will be purposeful from the first; and the tentative outline will save you from missing some fact or opinion you should record, will save you from making notes on masses of information you later have no use for, and will enable you to keep your growing collection of information in some sort of manageable order as you work. Any one of those results would justify the initial difficulty of thinking about your problem in advance. All together, they offer overwhelming reasons for making out a tentative outline as early as you possibly can and expanding or contracting it as your work shows the need.

EXERCISE

Submit to your teacher the tentative outline you have prepared to guide your reading and note-taking.

Reading and Evaluating Sources

Your purpose in reading is to find the answers to the questions you have asked yourself about the subject, to discover new questions, and to fill in the detail which will develop the topics in your tentative outline. It is usually well to begin with a book or an article written for the general reader rather than for the specialist, particularly if the subject is one that you know little about. The popular book or article probably will yield little that you can use in your final paper, but it will from the first give you a picture of the main outlines of the subject you are beginning to study. As a popularized book, it may well present a superficial and perhaps a distorted view, but your later reading will correct that, and just now it will tell you early in your reading what is generally known about the subject, so that as later reading fleshes out your understanding, you will recognize the importance of new details as you meet them. *Take no notes on the first book.* Later you may want to skim through it again and pick up anything of importance in it, but it is a waste of time to make careful notes before you know what is important and what is not.

Your preliminary bibliography contains many books and articles that may or may not be useful to you. If you are working on Poe as a critic, for example, any book on Poe might provide information, but as you work you will find that most of them, perhaps, offer you little help. It is not necessary, however, to read every word of every book and article in your preliminary bibliography to find the helpful sources. Instead, by using the prefaces, tables of contents, and indexes of the books, and by skimming the promising sections of books and the promising articles, you can quickly eliminate useless sources and concentrate your attention on the useful remainder. Prefaces are often ignored, but usually the preface can be an invaluable aid to the reader. In the preface the author is very likely to sketch his approach to the subject and indicate his methods. He may present his reasons for employing a particular arrangement in preference to some other, and he is very likely to explain what he is trying to do in the book. Also, the reader can often see evidence of the author's particular point of view and can pick up warnings of whatever bias he should be aware of as he reads. Make use of prefaces. They are not as dull and unrewarding as many people suppose. Make use, too, of tables of contents and indexes. The table of contents may help you quickly to discover the sections of the book that contain the kind of information you need, or you may find that your phase of the topic is not touched by the book at all. If the book is indexed, your work is still further simplified. Remember that the author may have used key terms slightly different from the ones you have used; check all the possibilities that occur to you. With that precaution, you can usually go from an index directly to the parts of the book that concern you.

Articles, unfortunately, do not have prefaces, tables of contents, and indexes. They must be examined directly. But even here it is not necessary or wise to plod doggedly through every word in hopes that something will turn up. Skimming is an art that you should develop as quickly as you can. Remember all that you have learned about writing and make use of it in your reading. Look for statements of thesis, usually toward the beginning of books or chapters or articles. Look for summaries toward the end. Be alert to pick up topic sentences of paragraphs and larger sections. As you run your eye over a page, you will quickly spot the key terms of your subject. Skimming an article on Poe to see if it mentions his criticism, you will be especially aware of such words as *critic, criticism, critical,* and they will stand out on the page to warn you to stop and read carefully. Even if you find that the sentence says only, "This was a critical winter in the poet's life," you will not have wasted much time. Look for dates that cover the period you are interested in, or look for proper names that you know might appear in a discussion of your phase of the larger subject. Only when you find pertinent material should you begin to read with careful attention to detail.

When you do find valuable material, read carefully, bringing to bear everything you have learned about the subject. In the book or article that treats your subject, what is the thesis? What are the main parts? What is the writer's particular approach to the subject? What are the implications of what he is saying, or perhaps of what he is leaving out? Is he objectively looking for truth or is he riding a prejudice? Question him, argue with him. Get everything from the source that you can. Read actively and intelligently, not passively and limply.

As you read, you will begin to see why a research paper cannot be a mere rehash of one or two books. The writer of the first general book that you read seemed confidently to know all there is to know about the subject; yet the more you learn, the more you may realize how much he left out, and how many other ways there are of interpreting the facts he presented. The authorities will usually agree on the major facts, even though particular facts may come to you from one source and another. It is the interpretation of the facts and the approach to the subject that differ from one source to the next. As a writer approaches facts from his own point of view, he will see something in them that another man sees from a different angle—the presumed motives behind an action, for example, may change the whole meaning of the action. The movements of Richard of Gloucester, for instance, after the death of Edward IV may be read as those of a villainous usurper or of a loyal Protector of the Realm in the minority of his brother's son. Even the attempt to present the facts themselves is often colored by the viewpoint of the beholder. Read, for a very interesting illustration, the eyewitness accounts of a battle from opposite sides. The Union colonel who seized Little Round Top at Gettysburg and the Confederate colonel who attempted to seize it were both convinced that the other side heavily outnumbered them. The two reports seem to be talking about completely different engagements. No wonder that the historians who have to try to find truth from such evidence come up with conclusions that differ. Your task is to weigh the evidence, consider the sources, and reach your own conclusions in the best light of your own intelligence.

(There will come a time in your reading when you feel an impulse to say, "Everything I'm reading says the same thing all the rest say." Resist the impulse. It means only that you are still reading popular or general sources. Go back to the indexes and dig deeper.)

You will not, of course, settle the questions for all time, but you have one advantage over the writers who preceded you: You are the latest in the field and can profit by their mistakes. One man has corrected another, and the third and fourth and fifteenth have corrected all of their predecessors. Each has introduced new facts or new ways of looking at the facts. You have a chance to use all the available evidence and may well come a little nearer the truth than anyone else has done.

There are certain tests that should be applied to each source as you read. First, who is the authority you are consulting? Find out all you can about him in the biographical dictionaries, or the membership rolls of learned societies, or the lists of the faculties of his college, or the card catalogue listing his other books, or wherever information may turn up. The Research Professor at the greatest university may not be the best man in the field, but he probably is not the worst. The writer of many books on a subject may be more dependable than a tyro—or he may not. Second, what do other authorities think of his work? The *Book Review Digest* will often tell you, or the specialized periodical indexes will lead you to reviews of his work. Third, *when* was the book or article written? The latest source is certainly not always the best, but an early one may well be out of date. Other things being equal, work with the most recent sources. Fourth, how much does the writer you are consulting know about the subject? The more you yourself learn about your subject, the easier it becomes to recognize superficial work. Fifth, how clear and how detailed are the evidence and the argument he offers to support his contentions? Do his theories cover all the facts, or has he ignored some inconvenient fact that might upset them? Are his explanations as simple as the circumstances permit, or has he built an unnecessarily complicated case? Finally, is he in general agreement with other authorities, or in violent opposition to them? Remember that the rebel might be right. The first man to say that the earth travels around the sun was closer to the truth than all the authorities who agreed that the sun travels around the earth. But the burden of proof is on the man with the new idea, and his evidence and argument must be scrutinized with a skeptical, although open, mind. Apply these tests to all your sources, weighing and evaluating as you read, using all your intelligence to come as near as possible to probable truth in your final conclusions.

Taking Notes

As you read, you will find yourself constantly coming across new facts, and, particularly, new ways of looking at the old facts. Take careful notes on everything new to you and important to the subject, so that when you write your final paper you will know whom to credit for the ideas you are borrowing.

Notes, like the preliminary bibliography entries, should be taken on cards so they can be rearranged, added to, and otherwise shuffled at will. Facts, important opinions, and pertinent questions will come to you in the order determined by the purpose of whatever authority you are consulting. They would soon be hopelessly jumbled if you tried to keep them on the pages of a notebook. Instead, use four-by-six-inch cards (large enough to give you room but not too large to handle easily) and *take one note to a card*. If an item is related to two or three of the topics in your tentative outline, fill out a card to be filed under each topic. This extra effort will seem like unnecessary trouble at the time, but it is far worse to know at the last moment that somewhere you have a note you need, if you could only find it. Here, as everywhere else in the research paper project, the more pains you take at each stage of the work, the easier the final task becomes.

As you take each note, record its source carefully, so that you will know later exactly where you got it. It is not necessary, however, to write down author, title, and the facts of publication on every card. If you are using only one book, for example, by Joseph Wood Krutch, all you need to identify the note is "Krutch," and the page or pages on which you found the item. Later, your bibliography card will provide you with all the additional information you need. If you have two sources by the same author, use a short title to identify each one. If you have two authors with the same last name, use initials. And so on.

At the top of the card, write the topic from your tentative outline under which the item belongs. That way, no matter in what order you discover useful material, you can always keep related details together, and from the beginning will have your material at least loosely arranged in manageable form.

A typical note card looks like this:

Daniel, p. 62   Chamber Tombs: Distribution

"Single chambers occur in two areas" of south-west Iberia: Almeria (circular, dry wall or orthostat wall); central and northern Portugal ("polygonal megalithic chambers"). Rectangular tombs rare in south-west, and when covered are round barrows. "... the long barrow... is non-existent in Iberia."

Most of your notes should be summaries of what your authorities are saying. Be sure your summaries are *your own words,* not thinly veiled quotations of the source. Take down in direct quotation only phrasings that are particularly striking, or statements for which you may later want the prestige of the exact words of a recognized authority. Such quotations as you do take must be copied exactly as they are in the text (spelled and punctuated, for example, as the original writer wrote them). They must fairly represent the author's intended meaning, not distort it when they are taken out of context. You may omit parts of the original, indicating the omission by the three dots of the ellipsis mark; you may insert explanatory material in square brackets; and you may use capitals and lower-case letters according to the final sentence pattern of your own paper. But you must be sure no distortion of the writer's original meaning results. Mark all quotations in your notes with quotation marks, to be sure you will later know exactly where paraphrase stops and quotation begins.

Except as aids to your own memory, you will not need source notes on details that are presented by virtually all the authorities, such as the birth dates of prominent people (on which all your sources will agree). But in your final paper, you will be expected to acknowledge your indebtedness for any details that have come, or that look as if they probably came, from particular sources, for individual interpretations of facts, for statistics or charts or tables you have borrowed from one of your authorities, and for passages you are quoting verbatim. For your own protection and convenience, record carefully the sources of all such material. You will need the information as you write the final paper.

Plagiarism Through Ignorance

It is important here to consider briefly the nature of summary and paraphrase and the problem of plagiarism. When a teacher, or a textbook, says, "Most of your notes should be summaries," or, "Mark all quotations in your notes with quotation marks to be sure you will know exactly where paraphrase stops and quotation begins," the matter seems so elementary and the injunction so clear that often no more is said about it. But when the final paper comes in, the teacher recognizes phrases and sentence patterns that are completely unlike the student's usual writing; no quotation marks indicate that the student is borrowing directly, although a footnote may acknowledge indebtedness for the ideas. When the teacher checks the source, he finds that the striking phrases and the uncharacteristic sentences come from the source, though perhaps with slight modifications. He calls the student in to examine the honesty of the paper, and often the student is genuinely bewildered. He has followed much the same procedures in earlier classes when writing précis reflecting the tone of the original: he has not copied the source word for word, quite; he has given credit to the source in a footnote. What has gone wrong? He may find himself in serious trouble without ever understanding why. (Sometimes, unhappily, he knows perfectly well.)

Just what does it mean to "use your own words"? We can best explain by using examples. William Gaunt, in a book entitled

London (New York: Viking Press, 1961), p. 25, wrote the following passage:

> Would you know how a merchant prince of the fifteenth century lived? In what stately surroundings, Crosby Hall, moved stone by stone and timber by timber from Bishopsgate to Cheyne Walk in 1908, can tell. . . . It is just as it was, . . . with its oriel window and oak roof, as when it belonged to a prosperous wool-stapler of the late Middle Ages; when after his death in 1475 it was occupied by Richard, Duke of Gloucester; and after 30 years again by Sir Thomas More.

Those are his exact words, and if they are used, they will of course be given a footnote to acknowledge the source. As a long quotation—say, over six lines—they will be indented and single-spaced, as in the sample page on page 53. The format means "this is quoted," so no quotation marks are needed. (A shorter quotation, with quotation marks, would be double-spaced and folded into the text, with the sentence patterns of the text adapted to the grammar of the quotation so that they fit smoothly together.)

There are several ways the passage may be used, *all calling for a footnote reference;* there is one way it may *not* be used.

1. It may be paraphrased. Using the names and the date and such key terms as *wool-stapler,* and in this case using the unavoidable chronological organization, you may say essentially the same thing in your own words and in your own way. It would not be indented in the paper:

> Crosby Hall, although it has been moved from Bishopsgate to Cheyne Walk, is unchanged from the days of its occupancy by a London wool-stapler who died in 1475, its occupancy after that by Richard, Duke of Gloucester, and thirty years later by Sir Thomas More. With its oriel window and its oaken roof it is a fine example of the home of a wealthy merchant at the end of the Middle Ages.

Because the idea and the information came from Gaunt, the paraphrase calls for the same kind of footnote as the direct quotation.

2. It may be summarized:

> Crosby Hall, successively occupied by a wool-stapler
> who died in 1475, by Richard, Duke of Gloucester,
> and by Sir Thomas More, exemplifies the houses of
> wealthy fifteenth-century merchants.

A footnote is still necessary.

3. Part of the information may be borrowed as fact:

> Sir Thomas More lived in Crosby Hall, in Bishopsgate,
> about 1505.

A footnote is still necessary, unless your topic is such that the same information can be found in most of your sources.

4. Part of the phrasing may be borrowed directly:

> Crosby Hall shows the "stately surroundings" in
> which "a merchant prince of the fifteenth century"
> lived.

A footnote is still necessary.

The only way in which it may *not* be used, the way which raises strong suspicion of an intention to gain for oneself the credit for organization and phrasing that rightfully belongs to William Gaunt, is to adopt his wording with only slight modifications:

> Would you like to know how a merchant prince of
> the fifteenth century lived? In what stately surround-
> ings, Crosby Hall can tell. It is just as it was, in-
> cluding its oriel window and oak roof, as when it
> belonged to a prosperous wool-stapler; when it was
> occupied after 1475 by Richard, Duke of Gloucester;
> and after thirty years more by Sir Thomas More.

No footnote can prevent the reader from thinking that you must have known that the sparkle in that passage, as well as the facts, belonged to Gaunt.

Unless you are careful as you take notes to mark all direct quotations clearly, you may not know, later, what phrasing is your own and what belongs to your sources. Your teacher may well regard the matter as very serious.

The Final Outline

When the investigation is finished—the sources combed, the facts and opinions collected, your questions about the subject answered—it is time to sit down and think about what you have learned. You are now, in some measure, an authority on the subject yourself; at the very least, you know a great deal more about it than the other members of the class. Your task now is to present what you have learned in such a way that a generally educated reader can understand it and learn from it too. Before you can write a clear paper, you must be sure you have not merely swallowed, but have also thoroughly digested, the material. A successful research paper cannot be merely a hodgepodge of undigested facts, nor an aimless stringing together of impressive quotations, nor a rambling presentation of interesting but unrelated remarks about the topic. It must be a clear, unified, and coherent paper about the subject you have been studying.

The tentative outline has enabled you, as you worked, to keep the material in some sort of order, and with luck you may have hit from the first on the best order possible. But re-examine that order now with the needs of the final paper in mind. The tentative outline represented what you at first thought you might discover. Additions and changes have had to be made as you worked, and now you know a great deal about the subject. What have you learned? What thesis would best summarize your new knowledge? What main points will you have to present and develop in order to clarify that thesis? Try various combinations as you attempt to beat the material into shape. It is time to expand your tentative topic outline into a formal sentence outline which will show you and your teacher that you have really passed the collected information through your brains and understand it thoroughly.

The outline for the final paper should be a full and formal sentence outline, using full declarative sentences at all levels. If you can get down on paper a clear and specific statement of thesis and can subdivide that thesis into main points which not merely indicate the topics you mean to discuss but say something definite about those topics, and if the progression of the resulting ideas is logical and clear, then you know that you have mastered the subject and that your thinking has been well done. Writing the paper itself will be easy, as by now it should be. Further, a full sentence outline enables your teacher to check your plans before you write. He can see exactly what you expect to say, and he has a chance to help you avoid any last-minute trouble. The research paper is probably the biggest single project of the year, and the grade counts heavily in your final standing in the class. If you and your teacher together can work over an intelligible sentence outline, he can usually suggest the chief difficulties you will need to watch for as you write. But he can do this only if he can understand exactly what you are planning to do. And only a sentence outline, made out in detail, will let both of you scrutinize your plans.

EXERCISE

Submit to your teacher your final outline, the cards on which you have listed your final bibliography, and the cards on which you have taken your notes.

The Final Paper

The final paper will consist of four sections: the title page, the outline, the text complete with footnotes indicating the sources of your detailed evidence, and the final bibliography. The third of these, the text, is obviously the most important of the four.

The title page should contain at least the title of your paper, your name, and the course and class.

The outline that accompanies the final paper may well be the sentence outline that served as a guide to the writing of the paper, or your teacher may require that that sentence outline be reduced to a carefully phrased topic outline. In either case, it is often useful to treat the final outline as a combined table of contents and index, indicating the pages in the text at which each idea is presented.

The text, the paper itself, is the heart of the project. The material in it has come to you from reading, rather than from experience; but the unity, the organization, the development, and the phrasing are your own. It is you who give meaning to the information you have accumulated. Except for indicating where you learned what you know, writing the paper is no different from writing any other paper. You need not try to work in all the evidence you have collected if honest and judicious selection can make your point just as well. You must not distort what seems to be the truth by ignoring inconvenient evidence, of course, but you may and should select the clearest and most pertinent. Since it is the most important single piece of writing done in the class, the paper on which you have spent the most time and the one dealing with the most complex material, bring to bear in writing it all you have learned about writing during the year. You should find, as a matter of fact, that it is also the easiest paper of the year to write. You know more about the subject matter than usual, you have given more thought to the development of the idea, and you have, besides, steeped yourself in the writing others have done on the same subject. Perhaps for the first time during the course, you can put your full attention on the actual writing job and can concentrate on phrasing your ideas in the most effective way, on making the clearest and most graceful transitions, on saying well the things you want to say. If you have done the work you should have done in preparation, you may be surprised and proud at the results.

FOOTNOTING: There is only one thing new about the text of the research paper: the necessity for using clear and conventional footnotes to acknowledge your indebtedness to the writers from whom you are borrowing details. It is not necessary or expected, remember, that you use footnotes to document details that might be found in most treatments of the subject. But it *is* necessary to use a footnote at any point at which you know that a particular source provided the fact, the opinion, the pattern, or the exact phrasing you are presenting. As you read, especially in the scholarly journals, notice how your authorities footnote their articles.[3]

Footnotes are conventionalized shorthand devices for saying to the reader, "I got the information I have just given you from so-and-so. He said it in his book or article with such-and-such a title. If you care to look into the matter further, you will find it on such-and-such a page." [4]

[3] There are in fact, many different systems, but the differences are matters of minor detail, such as punctuation. Most of them are based on the University of Chicago *Manual of Style,* and the pertinent forms may be examined in Turabian, *A Manual for Writers of Term Papers.* The form here recommended is that of the revised Modern Language Association *Style Sheet,* which is simpler and is now widely followed.

[4] That description applies to the most common type of footnote, the source note. There are also explanatory notes, like this one, which add useful information that could not gracefully be blended with the text. A third type of note combines the other two by citing a source and then adding explanatory comment.

That thirty-nine word remark to the reader can immediately be shortened to the name of the author, the work cited, the facts of publication, and the page, as in

Arthur Guilfoyle, The Ebb of the Confederate Tide at Gettysburg (Chicago, 1963), p. 327.

And there are a number of conventional abbreviations that make subsequent notes even briefer. See pages 46–47 for a full list. Here we may consider the most common. If the next note should refer again to the same work and the same page, the useful abbreviation *ibid.* (for the Latin word *ibidem*, "the same") will shorten your remark to the reader to those four letters alone. Or if another author's name and work intervenes, you may after the first reference to Guilfoyle's book use his last name only and the page, as in

Guilfoyle, p. 390.

A numeral after and slightly above the end of the detail you are documenting will announce to the reader that a note is appended; the same numeral at the foot of the page (before and slightly above the note) tells him which note to consult.
A sample passage would look like this:

some illegal trade, most of which probably came

from Lynn and Bristol in England.[16] During the

last years of the fourteenth century, however,

Greenland trade became unprofitable to Europeans.

African ivory, Russian fur, and Dutch and English

cloth had replaced Greenland commodities in the

European market, and the voyage to Greenland had

---

[16]Stefansson, Greenland, p. 160.

become increasingly risky.[17] The trade dwindled
and ceased.

About 1345, Ivar Bardarsson, steward of the
bishop's farms in the East Settlement, accom-
panied an expedition sent to find out why there
had been no news from the West Settlement for
several years. He found no human beings at the one
farm he stopped to investigate, but there were
cattle there, and sheep roamed about untended.
From this limited evidence he concluded that
the Skraelings (Eskimos) had recently slaugh-
tered the entire settlement.[18] In 1355, another
expedition was sent to find the missing
Greenlanders, but this expedition was unsuccessful
as well.[19]

After 1367, we hear little about the colonies.
In such isolation, life must have become more
unattractive and difficult.

---

[17]Norlund, p. 143.

[18]The story is told in Vilhjalmur Stefansson,
Unsolved Mysteries of the Arctic (London,
1939), pp. 28-29; Nansen, p. 127; Norlund, p. 134.

[19]Nansen, p. 128.

Typical footnoting problems are illustrated in the following samples. Note that the footnotes used in a paper are numbered consecutively or are renumbered with each page. Plan each page so that there is ample space at the bottom to accommodate the sources that must be cited on that page.

When writing a footnote, give the name of the author (first name first), the title of the book (underlined), the place and the date of publication (in parentheses), and the page number. Separate the items with commas, and put a period after each footnote.

A first reference to a book:

[1]William Carter, <u>Charles Dickens</u> (New York, 1964), p. 28.) *period*

A second reference to the same book and page immediately following the first reference:

[2]Ibid.

Another reference to the same book but a different page immediately following the first reference or an *ibid* to that reference:

[3]<u>Ibid.,</u> p. 328() *no period*

A first reference to a magazine article:

[4]Edward Wagenknecht, "Dickens and the Scandalmongers," <u>College English,</u> 11:374 (April, 1950).

Another reference to the same article and page immediately following the first reference:

[5]<u>Ibid.</u>

Another reference to Carter's book that was last cited in footnote 3:

op.Cit.
[6]Carter, pp. 42-44.

A reference to Wagenknecht's article, last cited in footnote 4:

⁷Wagenknecht, p. 376.

A reference, at secondhand, to something available to you only as a quotation by another source:

⁸Pieter de Haugen, Hoera de Koningin, as quoted by Edgar Gilbert, Modern Holland (The Hague, 1958), II, 269.

> [If you can examine the original source, you should do so; if one useful detail is there, others might be also. Footnote 8 also illustrates, incidentally, a reference to a work of more than one volume.]

An immediately succeeding reference to Gilbert's book cited in footnote 8:

⁹Gilbert, II, 297.

> [*Ibid.* could not be used here, since that would refer not to Gilbert, but to de Haugen.]

A reference to editorial material in an anthology:

¹⁰Stephen F. Fogle, "What Poetry Does," in A Brief Anthology of Poetry, ed. by Stephen F. Fogle, p. xi.

A reference to an unsigned newspaper editorial:

¹¹"Interstate Tax Chaos," Washington Post, June 18, 1964, p. A22.

A reference to an encyclopedia article:

¹²Morris William Travers and H. Grayson Smith, "Liquefaction of Gases," Encyclopaedia Britannica (1951), 14: 176.

> [The only difference between this first footnote reference and the bibliography entry is that the note cites the specific page to which reference is made, but the bibliography entry cites the inclusive pages covered by the article.]

A later reference, not immediately succeeding, to the same article:

13Travers and Smith, p. 180.

A reference to an authority personally consulted:

14Wood Gray, Professor of American History, The George Washington University, in a personal interview with the writer, February 27, 1964.

> [Such a note is rare, because a reader would find it difficult to consult the same source to check your accuracy or to obtain additional information. But an important point should not be omitted from your paper merely because it is not based on a published source, and if you consult an authority in person, you must credit him with the material he provides.]

A second reference to an author with more than one entry in the bibliography:

15Harrison, Over the Hill, p. 77.

> [The title must be repeated, since a reader referring to the bibliography could not easily tell which work had already been cited. If the note immediately preceding had referred to the same work, however, *Ibid.* would be perfectly clear.]

Other footnote problems will occur as you work, but if you remember that the purpose of the footnote is to inform your reader of the source of borrowed material, and if you understand the details of the method illustrated, you should be able to adapt your notes to the system.[5]

[5] The system presented is that commonly used by scholars in the humanities. The sciences frequently follow a different pattern, numbering their alphabetized bibliography items and making source references to those items by inserting in the text, in parentheses, the bibliography number and the page to which reference is made, as (17:39). Even science majors, however, will have occasion to write papers for advanced courses in the humanities, and the system illustrated in detail in the text should consequently be learned. Unless your teacher otherwise directs, follow the models in the text in your composition course research paper.

Abbreviations and symbols: The following abbreviations and symbols are conventional in footnoting. You will often see them in your sources, and you may have occasional need for them yourself. For any others that you find, consult your dictionary. (The underlined words are taken directly from a foreign language —Latin.)

above: appearing earlier in the same article. See *supra*.

art(s).: article(s).

below: later in the same article. See *infra*.

bk(s).: book(s).

c. or ca.: about, approximately; used with dates.

cf.: compare.

chap(s).: chapter(s).

col(s).: column(s).

ed(s).: editor(s), edition(s).

et al.: and others.

etc.: and so on. Not italicized, because it is now common English. But use it sparingly.

et seq.: and following; used of the pages following a cited page.

ff.: and following; used of the pages following a cited page. Now more common than *et seq.*

fig(s).: figure(s); used to refer to charts, diagrams, and so on.

ibid.: the same, used as a ditto sign to refer to an immediately preceding reference. May be used with a page change. When it is the first word in the footnote, as it usually is, it is capitalized.

infra: later in the same article. Not an abbreviation, it is not followed by a period. "Below" is now more common.

loc. cit.: in the place cited; used instead of *op. cit.* for magazine and encyclopedia articles, or for any source which is part of a larger, integral whole. Usage of *loc. cit.* varies, but this is its essential function. The author's name (or the title of an unsigned work) must accompany it. Often used with a page change.

MS(S).: manuscript(s).

n.d.: no date given.

n.p.: no place given.

n. pub.: no publisher given.

no(s).: number(s).

op. cit.: the work (opus) cited; used to refer to a previously cited book. The author's name and the page reference must always accompany it.

p. (pp.): page(s).

passim: here and there throughout. Used, rarely, to indicate that pertinent material is scattered all through an indicated work. Use specific pages wherever possible. No period because it is not an abbreviation, but a complete word.

sec.: section.

ser.: series

[sic]: thus in the original; used to indicate that an obvious error occurs in the source and that the quotation is exact. Used in square brackets, because it is a remark inserted in the quoted text. No period, because it is not an abbreviation.

supra: earlier in the same article. Not an abbreviation, it is not followed by a period. "Above" is now more common.

trans.: translator(s), translation.

vol(s).: volume(s).

Make use of these common abbreviations to save yourself the trouble of writing unnecessarily long footnotes. Since you will be expected to recognize and use these abbreviations in papers written for advanced courses, your teacher will not look with favor on long footnotes which appear to be attempting to evade the task of learning the use of the shorter forms.

THE FINAL BIBLIOGRAPHY: The final bibliography, the last section of your research paper, presents an alphabetized list of the sources you have found helpful in preparing the paper. All sources to which you have made footnote reference must be included, and it is often helpful to your reader to include any particularly good sources that you have not referred to directly. The bibliography thereby gives your reader a selected reading list on the topic you have studied. Practice differs here. Consult your teacher.

The forms of the final bibliography entries have already been illustrated in the discussion of the preliminary bibliography (pages 15–27). Consult those examples, and study the models offered in the attached student research paper. Follow the models exactly, in the order of details, in the information given, and in punctuation.

A FINAL WORD: You have a long, hard job ahead of you; there is no way in which digging information out of the library can be made painless. But if you follow the advice and the methods we have been discussing, and if you work intelligently and steadily throughout the time allotted to the project, you will find that it is not as hard as it may seem at first, and you will even discover, by the time you get into the intensive reading, that it really can be fun.

Examine the following typical student research paper for its methods of unifying material gathered from varied sources, its development of its topic, and its use of documentation.

THE PROBLEMS OF SLUMS
AND URBAN BLIGHT

by
James A. Ince

English IV
Mr. Sweeney
January 12, 1965

Underline Key words

<u>Thesis</u>: The problem of slums and urban blight, having identifiable causes and obvious ill effects, is now inadequately treated, but should be solvable by intensified, cooperative programs supported by governments at all levels and by the general public.

I. The age-old problems of slums have only recently received public attention.

II. Slums result from identifiable causes, some primary, others secondary.
   A. Primary causes are readily identifiable.
      1. Obsolescent, unattractive housing, allowed to deteriorate as it produces lower rental income, is of major importance.
      2. Other important causes are overcrowding, heavy traffic, industrial odors, and land speculation.
   B. Less important, secondary causes collectively constitute a problem.
      1. Physical causes are unsuitable building sites, inadequate street systems, and the shift of business to other locations.
      2. Economic causes are low incomes which chain people to slum areas, and the conflict between high urban property costs and low rental returns, which encourages owners to allow property to deteriorate.

i

III. The social and economic effects of slums
     are felt by the entire community.
     A. The social effects show in the high
        juvenile and adult crime rates and in
        the high disease and mortality rates
        resulting from overcrowding, filth, and
        lack of sanitation.
     B. The economic effects show in the high
        cost of fire and police protection and
        of relief and medical care, which must
        be borne by taxpayers in non-slum areas.

IV. Present redevelopment efforts often give
    more attention to slum clearance than to
    slum prevention, and defeat the purpose of
    providing low-cost housing because of the
    need to make privately financed projects
    economically profitable.
    A. Present efforts, by giving insufficient
       attention to satisfactory zoning and to
       the relocation of slum dwellers, often
       create new slums in clearing old ones.
       1. Insufficient attention to such
          matters as the use of space, sep-
          aration of industrial and residen-
          tial areas, and desirable housing
          standards results in developments
          which are themselves future slums.
       2. Eliminating overcrowded housing
          without providing for the reloca-
          tion of displaced residents creates
          more overcrowding in other slums.

ii

B. Private financing of redevelopment projects requires high rents to be profitable and thus defeats the purpose of
   providing low-cost housing for residents
   of the slum area being cleared.

V. Solution of the problems of slums depends
   on cooperative efforts by governments at all
   levels and by the general public.
   A. Federal assistance for local redevel-
      opment projects is already available
      and must be continued.
      1. Since 1949, federal loans to local
         governments have provided up to
         two-thirds of the cost of redevel-
         opment by private enterprise under
         the supervision of local government.
      2. The federal government also provides
         loans to build and subsidies to
         maintain low-cost housing develop-
         ments constructed, owned, and oper-
         ated by local governments.
      3. Because of inadequate local revenue,
         federal assistance will continue
         to be necessary.
   B. Municipal and state governments should
      accept more responsibility for the
      clearance of present slums and the pre-
      vention of future slums.
   C. The general public should actively sup-
      port slum clearance projects and insist
      on adequate housing standards.

iii

THE PROBLEMS OF SLUMS AND URBAN BLIGHT
James A. Ince

The problems arising from slums and urban blight are not new; they have probably been with civilization for as long as there have been cities. At least, references to slums and related problems have been found in the earliest written histories.[1] The major factors responsible for slums are varied and intermingled, a combination of social and economic problems.

> The slum is a residential area (comprising one or more lots, city blocks, or rural plots) in which the housing is so deteriorated (through poor upkeep ordinarily combined with obsolescence, age, depreciation, or change in consumer demand), so substandard (owing to builders' or owners' ignorance of principles of construction, planning, equipment, and hygiene, or to the deliberate ignoring of such principles), or

---

[1]Harold M. Lewis, Planning the Modern City (New York, 1949), II, 17.

so unwholesome (owing to narrowness of
streets, crowding of buildings upon the land,
or proximity of nuisances such as noxious
factories, elevated railways, overshadowing
warehouses, railroads, dumps, swamps, foul
rivers, or canals) as to be a menace to
the health, safety, morality, or welfare of
the occupants.[2]

This definition by no means encompasses all

the factors that produce slums, but it is com-

prehensive enough to indicate the scope of the

problem.

Although slums have been with us since the

beginning of history, only in comparatively recent

times has the general public become fully aware

of the deplorable conditions existing in these

areas.[3] This condition is due in part to the

---

[2]James Ford, Slums and Housing (Cambridge,
Mass., 1936), I, 13.

[3]Lewis, p. 19.

concept of democracy as it has developed over
the past two centuries. To say that a child raised
in a slum area has equal opportunity with a child
raised in more favorable surroundings is absurd.[4]
The foul atmosphere in which a slum child is
raised saps his vitality, corrupts his morals,
and usually leaves him with a hostile attitude
toward society. It thus materially reduces his
chances of becoming a well-adjusted and useful
member of society. Another reason for public
awareness is our rising standard of living, which
has widened the gap between slum dwellings and
the average home. This consciousness of the wide
difference between the living conditions of different segments of our population is being man-

_____

[4]Ibid.

ifested in legislation by federal and local

governments for the redevelopment of blighted

areas. Examples of such legislation are the

Housing Act of 1949 and the subsequent amendment

in 1954, with major emphasis on the prevention of

slums and blighted areas.[5] In order to eliminate

slums completely, we must first eliminate the

factors responsible for our blighted areas. It

will be necessary to make detailed studies of the

causes and effects of slums. The redevelopment

problems will have to be studied and solutions

recommended. Most of all, there will have to be

cooperation between the federal government, local

governments, and the general public.

The factors responsible for slum conditions

---

[5]Ibid.

can be divided into the broad categories of pri-

mary and secondary causes. Obsolescent housing

is an important primary cause of slum conditions.

With the advance of design and technology in

building houses, the old structures are no

longer attractive to most tenants. As it becomes

increasingly difficult to keep tenants in these

obsolete buildings, the rents are usually lowered

and buildings allowed to deteriorate because it

is no longer profitable to keep them in good

repair.[6] Other important factors are overcrowd-

ing, development of heavy traffic, noxious indus-

trial odors, and uneconomic use of land.[7]

     Finally the important factor of land spec-
ulation is a cause of blight, in that prop-

_____

[6]Ibid., p. 36.

[7]Ford, I, 446.

erties are held for prices at which there
is no possibility of appropriate and economic
development in the location. The speculator
anticipates sale for a higher-value use than
exists, and so reduces his expenditures for
maintenance to a minimum. He is not interested in the property as presently used
in the existing community, hoping to make a
profit on his invested capital by sale. The
tragedy of this practice is that there is
little or no possibility of such sales except
in isolated and fortuitous cases; yet each
such high-priced sale is used by scores of
owners in the neighborhood as an indication
that they also may expect a windfall.[8]

The secondary factors responsible for slum

conditions are not very important individually,

but collectively they constitute a major problem.

Some of these factors are physical, such as

unsuitable building sites, inadequate street

systems, or the shift of a city's business dis-

trict to a new location.[9] Other secondary factors

---

[8]Lewis, p. 36.

[9]Ibid., p. 35.

are mainly economic. Incomes that are too low

to provide money for adequate housing chain

people to slum areas.[10] On the other hand, high

costs, including taxes and mortgages, which are

not in keeping with the earning ability of an

area may cause its abandonment and subsequent

deterioration.[11] The two causes interact dis-

astrously. The effects of these various factors

which tend to bring about slum conditions are

felt not only by the individuals directly con-

cerned but also by the entire community as the

blight spreads.

There are, of course, other bad effects

within the slum itself. Slums in general have a

---

[10]Robert E. Alexander and Drayton S. Bryant,
Rebuilding a City (Los Angeles, 1951), p. 6.

[11]Ford, I, 447.

higher juvenile delinquency rate than surrounding
areas. The lack of playgrounds and supervision
of children's activities in these areas aggravates
this condition.[12] Adult crime seems to flourish
more in blighted areas than in other sections of
the city. High disease and mortality rates are
commonplace in slum areas. Communicable diseases
are easily spread by the overcrowded conditions,
filth, and lack of adequate sanitation.[13] One of
the many studies made of the social effects of
slums should illustrate the magnitude of the
problems.

> The San Francisco Planning and Housing As-
> sociation made a study of two contrasting
> residential areas with results that students
> of the subject know to be common in all
> cities. The "clean bright" Marina area of

---

[12]Ibid., p. 448.

[13]Ibid., p. 376.

53 blocks and 12,188 people was checked
against the blighted area known as Geary-
Fillmore with 41 blocks and 13,750 people.
Marina had, in the period studied, 133 fires,
Geary-Fillmore had 251; Marina had 17
juvenile court cases, Geary-Fillmore had
100; Marina had 39 "police" cases, Geary-
Fillmore had 4,771; Geary-Fillmore had 36
times as many tuberculosis cases, 66 times
as many hospital cases, and three times as
many infant deaths as Marina.[14]

This is not an isolated example. Similar studies

in other large cities have found the same results

--crime, juvenile delinquency, and disease are

widespread in slum areas.

The social effects of slums on a community

are only part of the problem. The cost of fire

and police protection for blighted areas is ex-

ceedingly high, and these areas drain heavily on

the city treasury for such services as relief

---

[14]James Dahir, Communities for Better Living
(New York, 1950), p. 78.

and medical attention.[15] Without a doubt, if the

cost of social services for the entire city were

as high as the services for slum areas, the city

would go bankrupt.[16] Since the people living in

these sections of a city have low incomes, the

revenue to pay for the social services must

come from taxpayers residing in other sections.[17]

This inequality causes many people to move to

the suburbs, thereby lowering the city's already

faltering tax base.[18] If concrete proposals are

not made for the redevelopment of blighted areas,

this flight to the suburbs will continue to grow

in the years to come.[19]

---

[15]Ford, I, 431.

[16]Ibid.

[17]Alexander and Bryant, p. 1.

[18]Lewis, p. 35.

[19]Ibid.

The redevelopment of blighted areas is a
complex undertaking and requires a well-organized
and aggressive city plan. Often redevelopment
plans pay too much attention to slum clearance
and too little to slum prevention.[20] Sufficient
consideration is not given to such problems as
size of city lots, architecture, and recreation
areas. Little is accomplished by erecting developments that will be tomorrow's slums. Effective zoning is essential to any redevelopment
project. Industries should be near, but not in,
residential areas.[21] Considerable attention must
be given to housing standards. Each room of a
house should have adequate light and ventilation.
Minimum standards should be established for
sanitation and general cleanliness of buildings.

---

[20]Ford, I, 495.

[21]Ibid., p. 615.

These housing standards should be applied to
suburban communities as well as redeveloped urban
areas, because suburban developments that lack
adequate design and planning can easily become
slums of the future.22 ____ Park, Virginia,
located about thirty miles from Washington, D.C.,
is a good example of a poorly designed community
that is very likely to become a blighted area
within the next twenty years. The entire community consists of houses having the same archi-
tectural layout. They are small and poorly
constructed, and have the general appearance of
summer cottages. Many of the residents work in
Washington, D.C., and thus create crowded highways
leading to the city. Elimination of housing developments similar to ____ Park is one of the

_____

22Ford, I, 477.

major steps in preventing future slums.

One of the most difficult problems in re-developing blighted sections of a city is re-locating the displaced population. In almost every location where slums are torn down and replaced by new housing developments, there are more families in the slums than can be adequately housed in the rebuilt area.[23] Care must be taken that these displaced families do not move to areas already overcrowded. Because of the low incomes of these families, the only practical solution seems to be an expanded program of low-cost government housing.

Another major obstacle in the way of urban redevelopment is financing. Slum rehabilitation

---

[23]Coleman Woodbury, ed., The Future of Cities and Urban Redevelopment (Chicago, 1953), p. 517.

through private effort is usually economically

unfeasible. If private capital were used to

finance redevelopment projects, the rents of the

new buildings would have to be quite high.[24]

Using private capital would therefore defeat the

purpose of slum rehabilitation: to replace slum

areas with housing developments for low-income

groups.[25] As mentioned earlier, land speculation

is one of the main causes of high costs. Some

method must be found to obtain at a fair price

the urban land that needs redevelopment.[26]

Other high costs stem directly from our postwar

inflation, and little can be done about them.

The only way these financial problems can be

---

[24]Ford, II, 572.

[25]Ibid.

[26]Lewis, p. 38.

overcome and an adequate slum clearance program

can be carried out for the country as a whole is

through government assistance.

In fact, the federal government already gives

considerable assistance to local slum clearance

projects.

> In the Housing Act of 1949, the Congress
> declared, in part, that the general welfare
> and security of the nation and the health
> and living standards of its people require
> the elimination of substandard and other
> inadequate housing through the clearance of
> slums and blighted areas, and the realization
> as soon as feasible of the goal of a decent
> home and a suitable living environment for
> every American family, thus contributing to
> the development and redevelopment of com-
> munities and to the advancement of the
> growth, wealth, and security of the nation.[27]

Federal financial assistance is available to local

---

[27]Meyer Kestnbaum, "Twenty-Five Federal Grant-
in-Aid Programs," Final Report of the Commission
on Intergovernmental Relations (Washington, D.C.,
1955), p. 147.

governments to assist them in the clearance of slum areas and for future redevelopment of these areas. These programs are carried out by private enterprise in accordance with local plans. The federal government does make decisions on the acceptability of the plans, but local governments can proceed on most general matters without further approval.[28] The federal government provides up to two-thirds of the net project cost, and the local government must furnish the rest in the form of cash, land, public utilities, or site improvements.[29]

Another way in which the federal government aids local communities in the fight against urban blight is through low-rent public housing. Since

---

[28]Ibid., p. 148.

[29]Ibid.

the main economic factor compelling most families

to live in substandard housing is low incomes,

these housing projects are essential to the

elimination of slums. The housing projects are

constructed, owned, and maintained by local

housing authorities operating under state enabling

acts.[30] If the United States Public Housing

Administration determines that a community has a

need for low-cost public housing, it usually

grants a loan, which must be approved by local

authorities, for preliminary work. After the

housing is complete, the federal government

pledges a subsidy which will cover the difference

between operating expenses of the project and

the amount obtained in rent.[31]

---

[30]Ibid., p. 223.

[31]Ibid.

It appears that federal assistance will have

to be continued for an indefinite period. Local

governments are unable to raise sums of money

large enough to finance adequate slum clearance

programs because the federal and state govern-

ments have tapped available sources of revenue

to such an extent that little more can be added

to the tax burden.[32] While cities are unable

financially to undertake a large-scale renewal

program, however, most cities could accept more

responsibility for the prevention of slums than

they are presently willing to do.

> The shocking neglect of many municipal gov-
> ernments in failing to enforce and modernize
> existing housing and building codes has done
> much to bring about widespread conditions
> of urban blight and has resulted in govern-
> mental subsidies on an increasing scale.
> Local governments should accept responsi-

---

[32]Guy Greer, Your City Tomorrow (New York,
1950), p. 113.

bility for the broad goals of raising
housing standards, eliminating and preventing
slums and blight, establishing and preserv-
ing sound neighborhoods, and laying a
foundation for healthy community development. Local governments should recognize
the interrelationship of these activities
and should work continuously to improve
administrative and fiscal coordination among
all local agencies and programs involved
in planning, development and enforcement of
codes and ordinances, slum clearance, public
housing, and other related elements. [33]

State governments have also shirked their respon-

sibilities in the field of slum clearance. [34]

This is one of the primary reasons why the

federal government has been forced to enter the

field of public housing on such a large scale,

despite the fact that slum clearance ideally

belongs at the municipal and state levels. [35]

---

[33]Kestnbaum, p. 224.

[34]Ibid.

[35]Ibid.

Together with government assistance, fur-
thermore, slum clearance needs the support of
the general public. So that our governmental
units may plan expansion and renewal of our
cities effectively, it is necessary for the
private citizen to give his support.[36] The people of a community must let their elected
officials know how they feel about having a well-
planned community.[37] Groups of public-spirited
citizens can do much to prevent the occurrence of
slum conditions. They can encourage the im-
provement and upkeep of tenements and call on

---

[36]John Popham, "National Citizens Planning Conference," New York Times, June 11, 1957, sec. 1,
p. 26.

[37]Luther Gulick, "Five Challenges in Today's New
Urban World," American City, 71:149 (December,
1956).

homeowners with suggestions on how their prop-

erty can be improved. If they cannot secure

voluntary cooperation, they should report all

violations of the housing code and make sure that

city officials require property owners to clear

up all discrepancies. If enough private citizens

actively support slum clearance projects, the

job of ridding our cities of slums will progress

at a faster pace.

The success or failure of slum clearance and

urban renewal will ultimately depend on the suc-

cess of modern city planning techniques.[38] City

planning, like any large undertaking, requires a

great deal of teamwork. This is why it is im-

---

[38]Henry S. Churchill, "City Planning in the
United States," Encyclopedia Americana (1957),
6:718.

portant that government and private persons

cooperate to rid our cities of slums and blighted

areas. It should be the goal of everyone con-

cerned to see that adequate housing is as

available as our public school system--open

to the entire population.[39]

_____

[39]Lewis, p. 21.

Bibliography

Alexander, Robert E., and Drayton S. Bryant.
　　Rebuilding a City. Los Angeles: The Haynes
　　Foundation, 1951.

Churchill, Henry S. "City Planning in the United
　　States," Encyclopedia Americana (1957),
　　6: 718-26.

Dahir, James. Communities for Better Living.
　　New York: Harper & Row, 1950.

Ford, James. Slums and Housing. Cambridge,
　　Mass.: Harvard University Press, 1936.

Greer, Guy. Your City Tomorrow. New York: Mac-
　　millan, 1950.

Gulick, Luther. "Five Challenges in Today's New
　　Urban World," American City, LXXI (December,
　　1956), 148-57.

Kestnbaum, Meyer. "Twenty-Five Federal Grant-in-
　　Aid Programs," Final Report of the Commission
　　on Intergovernmental Relations. Washington,
　　D.C., 1955.

Lewis, Harold M. Planning the Modern City. New
　　York: John Wiley & Sons, 1949.

Popham, John. "National Citizens Planning Con-
　　ference," New York Times, June 11, 1957,
　　sec. 1, p. 26.

Tunnard, Christopher, and Henry H. Reed. <u>American</u>
<u>Skyline</u>: <u>The</u> <u>Growth</u> <u>and</u> <u>Form</u> <u>of</u> <u>Our</u> <u>Cities</u>
<u>and</u> <u>Towns</u>. New York: New American Library,
1956.

Woodbury, Coleman, ed. <u>The</u> <u>Future</u> <u>of</u> <u>Cities</u> <u>and</u>
<u>Urban</u> <u>Redevelopment</u>. Chicago: University of
Chicago Press, 1953.